THE MOTHER

Hanif Kureishi was born and brought up in Kent. He read philosophy at King's College, London. In 1981 he won the George Devine Award for his plays *Outskirts* and *Borderline*, and in 1982 he was appointed Writer-in-Residence at the Royal Court Theatre. In 1984 he wrote *My Beautiful Laundrette*, which received an Oscar nomination for Best Screenplay. His second screenplay, *Sammy and Rosie Get Laid* (1987), was followed by *London Kills Me* (1991), which he also directed. *The Buddha of Suburbia* won the Whitbread Prize for Best First Novel in 1990 and was made into a four-part drama series by the BBC in 1993. His version of Brecht's *Mother Courage* has been produced by the Royal Shakespeare Company and the Royal National Theatre. His second novel, *The Black Album*, was published in 1995. With Jon Savage he edited *The Faber Book of Pop* (1995). His first collection of short stories, *Love in a Blue Time*, was published in 1997. His story *My Son the Fanatic*, from that collection, was adapted for film and released in 1998. *Intimacy*, his third novel, was published in 1998, and a film of the same title, based on the novel and other stories by the author, was released in 2001 and won the Golden Bear award at the Berlin Film Festival. His play *Sleep With Me* premièred at the Royal National Theatre in 1999. His second collection of stories, *Midnight All Day*, was published in 2000. *Gabriel's Gift*, his fourth novel, was published in 2001. *The Body and Seven Stories* and *Dreaming and Scheming*, a collection of essays, were published in 2002. His screenplay *The Mother* was directed by Roger Michell and released in 2003. He has been awarded the Chevalier de l'Ordre des Arts et des Lettres.

THE MOTHER

Hanif Kureishi

faber and faber

First published in 2003
by Faber and Faber Limited
3 Queen Square, London WC1N 3AU

Typeset by Country Setting, Kingsdown, Kent CT14 8ES
Printed in England by Mackays of Chatham plc, Chatham, Kent

A CIP record for this book
is available from the British Library

ISBN 0-571-22192-0

2 4 6 8 10 9 7 5 3 1

CONTENTS

Hanif Kureishi (right) with director Roger Michell

AN ACT OF TRUST

An interview about *The Mother* with Hanif Kureishi
by Walter Donohue

WALTER DONOHUE *What was it about this story that made you think that it should be a film rather than a novel?*

HANIF KUREISHI I don't truly know why, but maybe it's because sometimes you're looking for a film. It comes to you: you see certain images, which are transformed later on by the director. In this case, you see a woman doing her shopping, her gardening, looking after her husband – an old couple's life. Then, later on in the story, you see how she has been transformed by the death of her husband, and by her relationship with the builder, Darren. I saw all of that – I saw the builder coming into the house, and so on. And I saw it all in images rather than in words – which sometimes happens.

Is it also partly because you felt that the sex that is at the centre of the story would be better depicted on screen rather than on the page?

Not necessarily. In a sense, sex is much harder to do in a film than it is on the page, because it's easier to move inside the minds of the characters with prose. Whereas with a film, you're a voyeur: you're looking from the outside, watching these bodies, and your relationship to them is as a spectator. So it wasn't necessarily that.

There was also the desire to work with a director again. I'd worked with Udayan Prasad on *My Son the Fanatic* and Patrice Chéreau on *Intimacy*. Then I wrote *The Body* and the stories that went with it. So I guess it was time.

At what point in a film project does the director get involved with your work as the writer?

Once I've got a rough idea of the whole thing and I can see the whole story. But it's still quite rough, in the sense that there's a lot of material there, and what you *know* is that the director is going to have a version of the material that is going to interest him. When you give a draft to a director, he's got to find something in it that sparks his imagination, or is already working in his mind – that this is a subject that turns him on, in some way. Then you work on the script with the director, and after a few weeks you begin to see what he's interested in. You see he's thinking about where he wants to shoot and what he's going to do on the set and what he wants from the actors, and this will be an expression of his personality. But he also sees something about your ideas that is important, and he works out how to use that. And you as the writer are going to have to persuade him to the interest of your own ideas, or you have to engage in his ideas, or it becomes a synthesis of both.

So it really is a collaboration, as you begin to figure out together what sort of film you can make, but also what sort of film you *can't* make, and the areas you can't go into. It's also an act of trust, in a sense – that the two of you are going to do this thing together, and believe that it is going to work out.

In the case of this script, Roger [Michell] was very involved with his own mother, and he could find a way into the film through that. So then it became his film, as it were: a film about his mother, as well as, let's say, my mother. Or about all mothers.

Was Roger's mother the same age as the mother in the film?

I think his mother had died just before I gave him the script. So he was in a 'mother mood', as it were. I think he had been thinking about her a lot. She had been bereaved and left alone for quite a while – a bit like my mother. There has to be something about the material that will appeal to the director's unconscious, or his taste or style. You might write a perfectly good thing and give it to a particular director and sometimes it just won't do anything for them at all.

But you wouldn't give your work to just any director. This is the second time you've worked with Roger, just as you've worked with Stephen Frears twice. So are there certain directors who you feel have a particular affinity for your work?

Yes, though I'm always looking for new people to work with, because what's interesting about being a writer in films – as opposed to being a director – is that all the films are different. *My Beautiful Laundrette* isn't like *My Son the Fanatic*. You can offer your work to somebody and it comes out in all these different versions, which is the result of collaboration. Patrice Chéreau wasn't someone I had worked with before, and he took my work and transformed it into something I rather admired.

I worked with Roger on *The Buddha of Suburbia*, which was one of the first things he did; and it's interesting how different *The Mother* is compared to *The Buddha of Suburbia*. *Buddha* is directed in a number of styles, you might say. You never know from cut to cut what's going to turn up next. The characters are different, too. But with *The Mother* he seems to have invented a new style. You can see that he's developing as a director, looking for new ways to visualise things. So, when we were making the film, I had no idea what it was going to look like or how he was going to use the frame.

Once Roger said he wanted to direct it, did you re-write the script in line with suggestions he made?

Roger wasn't available for ages – he went off to America to make *Changing Lanes*. But we worked on the script a lot: there was a lot of stuff concerning the past, but otherwise the story remained more or less what it was when I first wrote it.

Once it was cast, was there a rehearsal period during which you worked some more on the script?

We read it through with the actors, and then Roger and I continued to meet and tinker around with it. Once shooting began, Roger didn't want me around on the set – some directors don't like you being there, it puts them off. Whereas someone like Stephen [Frears] likes the writer to be there all the time – fiddling around, cutting and changing things all the way through – and you get used to working like that.

Did anything change in particular because of the way the film was cast? Did the actors show you aspects of the characters that you hadn't thought of before as you saw them working their way through rehearsals?

No, not really. When they rehearsed, Roger mostly stuck by the script. But what he tried to do was to make it more natural. My dialogue is quite taut and stylised, and there isn't a great deal of it. Some scenes were just a couple of lines. I think that as Roger shot the film, he wanted it to seem more natural, as if people were talking a lot as they do in life. And because they were such experienced actors, he encouraged them to improvise and to speak around the script, just chatter away to make it seem more natural, rather than having two or three lines which would stand in for the rest of it. So there's a lot of dialogue in the film that I actually didn't write, because of the style that we wanted.

Was there one aspect of the film more than others – a core theme, let's say – that drove you on in the writing?

The basis of the film, where I began from, was really the discussions between the mother and the daughter. And what I'd become interested in – mostly through therapy and psychoanalysis – was versions of the past, the way they both spoke about the past. How, when the daughter comes home from her therapy session and confronts the mother, the mother is completely bewildered by the daughter's version of the past. The daughter has got these new words that the mother has never heard before, and she doesn't understand what's going on. And they have this dispute because neither of them recognises the other's different version of the past. So I became very interested in children and their parents. These are stories that don't necessarily cross over at all – as if the two characters had inhabited a different world. But I'm also interested in therapy, and how that encourages you to tell alternative stories of your past that then might not be recognisable to your parents at all. So that's where it began – from the disputes between the mother and the daughter, which were at the centre of the film, and which I spent a lot of time trying to get right, in order to get the tone of the rest of the film right.

There are also disputes between the son and the daughter. At one point he says to her, 'You've always been jealous of me.'

What I was trying to get at was the way in which the past works in the present. You wouldn't have flashbacks of the past, you'd have them talking about the past, and the past would be alive now as it would have been then, except the words they use are dangerous and the characters clash over those words.

It's interesting that other writers and directors are contemplating this now. I'm thinking of [Thomas Vinterberg's] *Festen*, which was shot in a particularly casual way in order to capture the everydayness of people's lives. But then *Festen* was rather like Bergman's films, which tend to be almost entirely about the past or about people using the past in the present in order to say certain things, to take positions, to attack one another, to establish certain ideas about themselves. You might use the word 'abuse' in the widest possible sense, as in a parent dominating a child. In *The Mother*, you have the daughter coming out from under the child, as it were, and asserting herself against the mother. And that is very painful for the mother, which is why she steals her daughter's boyfriend.

Is there a danger, do you think, that the love affair comes to dominate the film and so the relationship between the mother and daughter gets lost?

I guess I was thinking of the family as a complete structure: so that when something happens at one end, it has a knock-on effect at the other. Rather like in Pasolini's *Theorem*, where someone walks into a family – in that case he has an affair with *everyone* in that family – and it affects the whole structure of that family. However, in *The Mother*, Darren is already *in* the family, with the daughter and the brother. And he then takes the mother as well – as if he's another son, trying to reclaim a place in the family.

And is it subconscious on the part of the mother to take Darren away from her daughter? Because of the challenge the daughter has thrown in her face?

Yes. In a sense, nobody knows quite what is going on, just as no one knows what's really going on in their unconscious. But they're living it out in some way, and that's what makes it tragic. There's no sense in which the mother does it deliberately – it wouldn't work so well if she did. She does what we call 'falling in love', which makes it more tragic, because it's their fate or their destiny rather than their choices that seem to determine their lives.

I think the film probably speaks to women of a certain generation whose lives were bound up with their husbands. If the husband was taken away, what they were left with was an empty house and a pair of slippers, and the feeling of, 'Is this what my life is?', 'Is my life now over?'

That's right. I guess feminism was the biggest revolution in my lifetime – I was brought up right in the middle of it. My mother – and the housewives in the suburbs we grew up in – their place was to look after the man. It seems to us now like a very strange idea, but that's what they did. When my dad asked my mum for a cup of tea, she went and got him a cup of tea – not necessarily because she loved him, but because that's what her place was in the system. And those women thought that they kept their place in the system by bringing up children and looking after the husband so that he could work. So the idea of a woman who would make her life, her destiny, outside of what was expected of her, as an individual, was quite unusual then.

The daughter says that she has to work and bring up her child on her own, while, in her mind, the mother has had a comparatively easy life.

Well, the daughter's life is harder because she decided to go it alone. She's a teacher, and a single motherm, so she envies the mother, who was a housewife, and presumably had a certain amount of money, and a house – which seems to the daughter to be luxurious. And of course, the mother also had a husband who was always there, while the daughter doesn't. On the other hand, the mother would envy her daughter and her life in London. So each of them envies the other, and I wanted to take these two generations of women, who were both privileged and not privileged, and bring them together.

Where does the son fit into all that?

Well, the central characters were the mother, the daughter and the lover. And then there were subordinate characters around that – and further out, there are other small characters. The son is a modern man who's trying to do well and be successful. He's also trapped; you realise how trapped you are when your money starts to fail you. He believes in the whole dream of making money, supporting his family, accumulating things. But it's beginning to fall apart and he's in some distress about it. He clearly doesn't have much time for his mother.

But he's also not traumatised by his relationship with his mother in the way his sister is.

On the surface, he's much more together than the daughter is. She is clearly falling apart psychologically, but then you might say she's better off than him, in that she can at least express it. Her stress is much more on the surface – she's trying to write – whereas he's much more of a 'man', and his distress doesn't really manifest itself. He's really keeping it together. So I wanted to compare these two lives as well. Which do you prefer? Do you want this smooth, cool, outwardly together guy? Or do you prefer someone who seems more hysterical?

The fact that she is hysterical is admitting that a problem does exist, rather than burying it under a smooth surface.

One of the things that happens with your parents is that you fall out of love with them. You have this very intense love affair with your parents as a child – it probably goes on for thirteen or fourteen years – and after that it begins to fall apart. And it falls apart for ever, you might say. The daughter is trying to come to terms with that in some way, mostly because she's had therapy and she sees that it's important.

It may also by that the son was indulged by the mother, whereas the daughter wasn't.

That may be so. But also the son is trying to subsume his conflict, his desire, into materialism. There was a long speech in the film that Roger cut out, in which the son talked about how owning things was how he expressed himself. So he wanted to buy more carpets, more houses, more things. And the daughter would say, 'Well, that's just materialism', whereas his argument is that throughout history people always expressed themselves through their possessions – through their houses, their children, their wives, their land, their horses; this was not a new idea, people had always done it. But, of course, the sister would have found that contemptible.

The danger is that if that speech were in the film, it would be too on-the-nose. I think you can tell from the film as it is now that the son has committed himself to a materialistic way of life and that he takes it for granted.

And he's not a fool. I don't think that he believes it in the most fatuous way; it's just one way of living in the world for him. This is something to believe in, which people have believed in for a long time and which therefore might be worth believing in because of that. You extend yourself through ownership, and that's your power. Just as a woman might believe that she extends herself through her children. So these may be versions of being male and being female.

In Theorem, *the way that Terrance Stamp makes his way through the family is somewhat schematic. How did you avoid making Darren seem like that?*

I guess because he was already embedded in the family. In *Theorem* Terrance Stamp turns up at the beginning of the film, walks through the door, and disturbs everyone. I wanted to start further in on the story, so that you could see that Darren was already there, and *then* he disturbs everybody. So you have this family that is complete – a mother, father and two children – plus this other character, who's a friend of all of theirs, in there as well.

Look at the father – he only meets Darren very briefly at the beginning, but he starts talking to him about something, immediately drawing him into the family. Whereas the mother walks away from them across the garden, the father engages with Darren as if he is some long-lost son.

I was interested in Darren's place in the family: what he was going to do, how he was going to break things up – partly through his sexuality, but also through his friendship with the son. In a sense, he stood in for the wilder parts of the others that were repressed, the sexual parts of them. So you have this uptight, ordinary bourgeois family – lower-middle class, I guess – with this guy in it who's clearly disturbed and addicted and wild, and he represents or stands for the bits that they really can't *bear*.

Darren was beginning to destroy them, but at the same time he's aware that he's being used by the family; they've always represented it as being him that's getting a lot from them rather than the fact that it's really the family getting a lot from him.

I was also interested in the way families as complete systems tend to draw other people in, and give them a function, as a way of avoiding being completely incestuous. But then no one necessarily knows exactly what's going on in this saga.

It's almost as if the father wanted to have two sons – one who was aggressive and successful but not particularly physical, and another who was physical and athletic, to whom he could talk about cricket.

It's interesting how often parents want their children to do better than they do, in the way that my father wanted me to do better than him. Clearly, that would be a good thing for a parent to want in a child. On the other hand, after a bit, parents no longer recognise their children as being part of them. The children are so different, it's so startling, and there is no longer a relationship. In a way, the parents have wished the children out of the family circle, and that's quite disturbing because you've pushed them out of your class, as it were. And then you no longer recognise them. A lot of drama in the 1960s was about that – about working-class people trying to succeed in Britain, and how you succeeded to the extent that you lost your children.

What happened to the film once shooting was finished and you entered the editing stage?

Well, there's a point where finishing the film becomes rather functional: you're just looking for the good bits that you've shot, because, however important one bit may be in the story, if it doesn't work very well, if it's not shot very well, or if the actors are not doing it right – you have to take it out. So you put all the good bits in a line: that's what finishing the film is all about. And then the film starts changing. It's interesting how it happens, how the emphasis in the film changes, how the characters change.

Can you give me an example of where the finished film was different to what you had expected?

Roger may not like me saying this, but it returned to what it was originally – although there was much more dialogue in the original script. More explanation, I guess. But that kind of material is really there for the writer to inform the director about what the film is really about.

It's pretty much as I imagined the film would be, I guess – rather still and slow. I didn't want it to be a quick, fast, bright, modern film with a lot of cutting and loud music and pace. I wanted it to be rather slow and dreamy. I wanted it to gradually draw you into the lives of these characters, so you'd sit with them and get involved with them. I wanted a film that would test your patience, so you would wonder: where is this going to take me?

There's always talk of film being a 'director's medium' – do you agree with that, and with the corollary that this film is not 'yours'?

Well, all the films I have done have been collaborations. There are some directors who can write their own films, such as Bergman, but most directors are not writers. And no matter how beautifully a film has been shot, in the end it's the story that compels people. Most people don't watch a film just because of the images. On the whole, it's the story that pulls you in: what's going to happen next to the character? And that is decided by the writer who designed the character originally.

In Britain, there is a tradition of the writer and director working together. Film and television are very much writers' media here. Particularly when I was growing up, you'd see something because it was written by Dennis Potter, or Alan Bennett, or Alan Bleasdale or Alan Plater or Harold Pinter. Pinter's films with Joseph Losey are a perfect example of collaboration – it's impossible to say who's doing what in those films. That is the tradition I came out of, which I rejoined after working at the Royal Court with Stephen Frears, who placed an enormous importance on the place writers have in this process.

I guess the difference between the UK and the US is that in the US writers know there is a formula that you have to write within, which means that any director can direct it; whereas in Europe, the writer has a particular vision, so that it's a question of finding a director who can respond to this vision.

To find a director to do my scripts, there are certain interests you'd look for, a certain background – which, in Roger's case, was his having worked at the Royal Court. There'd be things that you would have in common, certain ideals – for one, that you'd try to make a film that is as good as it can be, without necessarily thinking about how much money it would make at the box office. Our ultimate aim is to make a film that we're both pleased with, no matter how well or badly it does commercially.

Going back to the idea of collaboration – the culmination of all those who collaborated with you is now up there on the screen, and seems to have produced something that is much like what you imagined when you first wrote the script.

And that's particularly because of Ann Reid being so wonderful in the title role. I try to write good parts for actors – these are big parts, there is a lot they can do and they're going to be on screen for a lot of the time – like the father in *My Son the Fanatic* or Anne in this film. You know when you're writing it that these are really big parts and you need tip-top actors. You don't necessarily know who they will be, but you have to believe that someone will turn up, and without that it won't work. If Ann Reid hadn't been good in this film, it would have been hopeless. So you have a certain amount of trust that you're going to find good British actors who are going to be able to play these parts and who will be bringing a lot of other things to the part which you hadn't anticipated. You take the risk. But that's absolutely the pleasure of it: that someone's going to turn up and be so amazing in your film that it's going to make the whole thing gel. And that's an act of trust.

Spring 2003

The Mother

CAST AND CREW

INT. SUBURBAN HOUSE BEDROOM. DAY

The house of May and Toots, a couple in their mid-sixties.

They are in bed. She watches the numbers on the clock change until, suddenly, the alarm goes off.

It's 5.30 a.m.

Her hand reaches out to turn it off.

INT. SUBURBAN HOUSE BEDROOM. DAY

Toots sits on the bed, naked apart from his vest, as May puts his socks on. He farts as she leans forward. She turns her head away and makes a face.

> TOOTS
> I'm going to be sweating like an old donkey.

> MAY
> You know how windy it gets in London.

INT. SUBURBAN HOUSE KITCHEN. DAY

Toots and May are in their coats, ready to go, sitting at the kitchen table. The doorbell rings.

INT./EXT. SUBURBAN HOUSE HALL. DAY

May bends down to take off Toots's slippers, putting on his day shoes. She places his slippers carefully beside the door, ready for his return. In the background we can see a minicab and driver waiting.

> TOOTS
> (*voice over*)
> Get on, woman!

5

INT./EXT. MINICAB. DAY

*Dirty; a loud radio. May and Toots sit in the back, bags on their knees,
their heads barely visible above their cases.*

TOOTS

He's got three bathrooms.

DRIVER

He must be clean!

TOOTS

He's a clever boy, you see.

EXT. SUBURBAN RAILWAY STATION. DAY

*May and Toots climb the stairs to the platform. Toots, sweating and
breathing heavily, stops and puts his case down. It slips back down the
stairs. They turn and watch it go.*

Wearily, May starts to go back for it.

TOOTS

Hurry up! We're going to miss the blasted train!

INT. INTER-CITY TRAIN. DAY

She unwraps some sandwiches.

MAY

Here.

TOOTS

What is it?

MAY

Don't worry about that.

TOOTS

I do worry about your food.

*She holds a sandwich at his mouth and he nibbles reluctantly at it.
She keeps holding it there.*

I don't want it.

INT./EXT. LARGE LONDON STATION. DAY

They emerge onto the concourse. Rush hour. They look around for the entrance to the Tube. The station looks vast and confusing.

EXT. GOLDHAWK ROAD. DAY

They come out of the Tube. The street is busy. They can't get their bearings.

EXT. NOTTING HILL STREET. DAY

An exhausted Toots and May turn the corner into a rather grand residential street and look across at a large house. May has an address on a scrap of paper in her hand.

They stand there, hovering about, unsure of themselves.

TOOTS

Which one is it?

MAY

That one, I think.

Pause.

Come on. They invited us.

INT./EXT. BOBBY AND HELEN'S HOUSE. DAY

Helen opens the door in her dressing gown to see Toots and May standing there.

Helen is in the middle of towelling her hair, but she tries to be polite and even enthusiastic.

TOOTS

It's us!

He kisses Helen. She laughs with pleasure and embraces them both.

HELEN

Hi! Hello, you both. My God, you're so early! Come on, come in. It's so great . . . you're here, at last! Bobby's been so looking forward to this . . .

Kids shriek behind her. Helen turns back into the house, distracted by the kids. May and Toots pick up their bags and walk into the confusion.

(*to kids*) Yes, yes, I'm coming, stop asking for things in that whining voice! Just give me five minutes to get ready! Some of us have to go to work!

As Toots and May follow Helen into the house, Darren, a builder in his thirties, comes in behind them, struggling with a heavy-looking ladder.

DARREN

Mind your backs – mind your fronts – mind your minds and manners!

MAY

Oh dear!

All right!

TOOTS

I'm breathing dust in!

DARREN

Everyone hold your breath for ten minutes!

Still clutching their bags, they follow Darren into the big house.

MAY

It's like Buckingham Palace.

A young, nervous Au Pair with green hair is trying to prepare the older kids for school.

TOOTS

Hello, hello, hello, little ones!

HARRY
(*to Au Pair*)
Have they brought us presents?

ROSIE

What have they got?

Pause.

Who are they?

HELEN

Oh, for God's sake.

MAY

What a lovely house!

INT. BOBBY AND HELEN'S HOUSE. DAY

May sits on the sofa giving presents to the kids. The Au Pair is packing their school things in the background, as Helen harangues her on the exact way to pack a sandwich. Helen and Bobby have three kids, aged nine, six and six months.

Toots wanders around, examining prints on the walls, humming to himself.

9

MAY
(*as the two eldest rip into the gifts*)
You never know what to give people.

Harry is playing with a noisy game whilst listening to music on his headset.

What are you listening to?

HARRY
What?

MAY
What are you listening to?

HARRY
What?

ROSIE
You've got a broken face.

HARRY
How long are you staying?

Helen, who has changed, now comes into shot, putting on her jacket. She's carrying a briefcase and swathe of cashmere clothes over one arm.

HELEN
(*to Cleaner, ironing in the kitchen*)
Inside kitchen cupboards; beds, baths but not the children's; the fourth floor but not the third; and the ironing but not that blue dress which I want re-washed, for reasons that will become obvious . . . (*to Au Pair*) After school you can take them to the park, but no dairy for Rosie, please, Sarah's going to Ella's, oh, and Geraint is coming here tomorrow, no Thursday . . .

Suddenly Toots gets up and dances with Helen, interrupting her spiel. She laughs and is charmed by him.

TOOTS
How graceful you are, my dear.

HELEN

Stop! Stop!

TOOTS

And elegant, always like a picture.

HELEN

Oh, Toots you're always sweet . . . I'm late! I'm late!

TOOTS

Where is he then? Still in bed?

HELEN
(*to Harry*)

Do not do that! (*to Toots*) He had an eight-thirty. He'll be
here in a second.

MAY

He's not overdoing it?

HELEN

We're all doing that.

TOOTS

Have you got a little job?

HELEN

Didn't he tell you? Didn't he call you? I've just opened the
shop!

MAY

Oh? Selling what?

HELEN

Cashmere, anything you can get made out of gorgeous
cashmere, look, just touch that . . .

She shows them a bundle of cashmere scarves.

TOOTS

You girls are doing everything now.

MAY

It's very soft.

Bobby hurries in, a little flustered, and greets everyone.

BOBBY

Dad. Mum – you got here okay. Nice and early too. I've just popped back to say hello.

MAY

Aren't you spending the day with us?

BOBBY

If only. God, I'd love that. I've got wall-to-wall bloody meetings all day.

MAY

Everyone wants him.

BOBBY

Yeah, that's it, Mum.

TOOTS

Then everything's going well? Business is good?

BOBBY

Er, yeah, business is . . . we're, busy, it's very –

HELEN

I've got to go.

BOBBY

Yeah, me too, I'll see you tonight? We're going to Paula's. She's cooking, so watch out!

HELEN

Please . . . make yourselves at home . . . use anything you want . . . there's some really nice basil risotto in the fridge –

BOBBY

Can I get a lift?

Bobby and Helen start to go out, picking up mobiles, kissing children, putting on clothes.

HELEN

As long as you don't talk to me.

BOBBY

Most of the time you criticise me for not talking to you.

HELEN

That's because you only talk to me when I'm trying to do something else.

Darren comes in with more gear. He and Bobby have a boys' mock fight.

(*to Bobby, about Darren*) Stop it. He's slow enough as it is. Michelangelo, took less time over the bloody Sistine Chapel.

DARREN
(*winking at May*)

This'll last longer.

And he goes off to the conservatory, the front door slams, the Au Pair shoos the kids to get their school bags and shoes on, and May and Toots are left pretty much alone.

Pause.

TOOTS

Basil risotto? What the hell is that?

INT. BOBBY AND HELEN'S HOUSE. DAY

Later. It is quieter now. May and Toots walk about the house, drinking tea. The exhausted Polish Cleaner continues to wash down the tiles in the corridor.

TOOTS
(*to Cleaner*)

Do you know the work of the poet Czeslaw Milosz?

She looks blankly at him.

Milosz? Czeslaw? Or is he Lithuanian? Or Polish?

MAY

Just because she's from Poland.

TOOTS

How about Miroslav Holub?

CLEANER
(*in Polish*)

I don't know what you're talking about, chum.

May looks through the French windows doors at the back of the house and sees Darren working on the new conservatory. He stops for a moment and smiles at her.

The Au Pair calls through to Darren from the kitchen.

> AU PAIR
> Darren, is it your cup of tea is up?

> DARREN
> I should think it is right up.

May walks through the half-done conservatory. As she does so, Darren is lighting a cigarette. She looks at him, about to speak, when she realises Toots has followed her out.

> Pleased to meet you, sir. Darren.

> TOOTS
> Toots. Do you like this work?

DARREN

I try to.

Toots inspects Darren's work with a knowledgeable and approving air.

TOOTS

Some of this is very careful work.

DARREN

Built to last. They'll be able to sit out here in their old age.

TOOTS

They won't enjoy it. They won't know what to do with themselves.

Pause.

This is Bobby's mum.

MAY

And Paula's. We have a daughter.

DARREN

I know.

Pause.

I'm probably Bobby's oldest pal. We were at college together, 'cept I left in the second week. He's been the greatest friend to me.

MAY

Has he?

TOOTS

Are you the man who did Paula's kitchen?

MAY

Oh, she was delighted. You must be Darren. She said you were – a man who can do everything.

DARREN

I'm doing her a study. Somewhere for her writing.

TOOTS

Yes. You know us all. Do you like cricket?

May walks out into the garden.

DARREN

Yes, yes. I do.

TOOTS

Playing or watching?

EXT. BOBBY AND HELEN'S GARDEN. DAY

May walks in the garden. She breathes in deeply. She looks at the two men talking in the unfinished conservatory, demonstrating cricket strokes to each other.

EXT. SHEPHERD'S BUSH GREEN. EVENING

They walk – May, Toots, Bobby and Bobby's eldest, Josh – through a much more run-down part of the city, past strange central European restaurants, rowdy pubs, minicab offices . . . Police cars rush past, sirens on.

17

Toots walks behind, holding the hand of his grandson, unable to breathe properly.

> BOBBY

Come on, Dad, it's not far.

He looks at his father, shocked.

> MAY

Not too fast, Bobby.

> BOBBY

Is he all right?

Toots holds out his other hand, which Bobby takes.

> TOOTS

I'm not ready . . . not ready . . .

> MAY

We should've taken the bus.

> BOBBY

I didn't realise he was –

> TOOTS

I'm not. I just want to see Paula.

INT. PAULA'S FLAT. EVENING

Paula and her eight-year-old son Jack are hastily chucking his toys behind the sofa. They shove it back against the wall.

Through the window we can see Bobby helping Toots down the steps into Paula's small, unkempt basement. However, Paula has gone to some trouble to lay the table in her living room. Candles; wine; napkins.

She goes to the door.

> TOOTS

My little ballerina!

> PAULA

Oh, Daddy – I'm so glad you've come up to see what we're all doing!

TOOTS

Still not married?

MAY

Leave that, Father.

PAULA

Once was enough.

TOOTS

The boy needs a man like me around the place.

PAULA

Bobby's going to introduce me to one of his rich friends –
aren't you, Bobby?

BOBBY

Darren's rather adept with his hands, I hear.

PAULA

Get lost!

TOOTS

It's my last wish that you look after your sister.

BOBBY

'Bout time she looked after herself.

MAY

Oh, sit down, and don't start arguing straight away.

PAULA
(to Bobby)

Look at this. Come on, have a look.

*Paula opens a door to show Bobby her 'study', a small box room which
contains mostly new wood piled against the wall. May now comes and
stands behind him.*

He's just left it like this.

MAY

Who has?

PAULA

Darren!

MAY

Tell him off! That's a rotten thing to do.

PAULA

Bobby's got him working all hours.

BOBBY

I'm paying him. It's not a favour. Jesus! I've got more than Darren to think about!

His mobile phone starts to ring. He walks with the phone off into the kitchen.

BOBBY

(*out of shot, on phone*)

I can't do that, no. We'll have to find another kind of deal. But that's okay . . . As long as we sort this out.

PAULA

Come on, Mum, rest your ankles.

INT. KITCHEN. EVENING

Paula is preparing supper.

PAULA

Aren't you going to take them out?

BOBBY

I'm up to my neck in it. They've come all this way. Can't you take them to a couple of museums or something?

PAULA

Why can't you look after them for a change?

BOBBY

They're staying in my bloody house, aren't they?

May comes in with some wrapping paper and finds the bin.

MAY

Please! Stop bickering, you two, your father's not well. (*May looks at them.*) Give me a cuddle, one of you.

Pause.

BOBBY

This is unusual, Mother. You haven't become a New-Ager, have you?

Bobby watches as Paula hugs her.

INT. PAULA'S LIVING ROOM. NIGHT

The family meal. They all sit around the cramped table. May watches Toots and wipes his sweating face with a handkerchief.

TOOTS

(*to Bobby*) She must keep on with her art, and never give up. To be fulfilled, people have to follow their deepest passion . . . That's something I've learned, doing the opposite . . .

Paula rushes through from the kitchen and puts the casserole on the table.

PAULA

Mind out! Careful everyone! It's hot!

Jack and Rosie cheer.

Paula sits down at last.

Here we are. All done at last. Now, let's eat!

BOBBY

Who wants wine?

PAULA
(*hisses at him*)
You didn't even bring any!

BOBBY
(*pulling the cork*)
Here it comes!

TOOTS

I'm so happy – happy to see everyone together! Like the old days! When we all drove to Scotland . . . and you were young, and we felt young . . .

PAULA

We were sick out of the car window!

TOOTS

And Mother wore summer dresses . . . and went pink in the face like a salmon!

MAY

Oh, Toots –

TOOTS

And it rained in sheets and buckets –

BOBBY

And we played table tennis –

PAULA

You read to us and when I wanted to make up my own stories, Bobby hit me!

BOBBY

No, no! No I didn't!

PAULA

He was always hitting me –

Laughing, he raises his fist to her.

MAY

Bobby . . .

TOOTS

You're the thing I'm most proud of . . . my children!

PAULA

Daddy . . .

May wipes her eyes.

TOOTS

And we . . .

He can't go on.

MAY

Yes, yes . . .

BOBBY
(*holding up his glass*)
To us all. Long lives. Good lives.

PAULA

Yes.

MAY

Oh yes, yes.

Their faces as they clink glasses.

INT. BOBBY AND HELEN'S SPARE ROOM. NIGHT

That night. May and Toots in bed in Bobby's house. Toots burps and holds his chest.

TOOTS

Paula's food always makes me feel ill. You should have told her what I like.

MAY

What shall we do tomorrow?

TOOTS

Can't we go home?

MAY

What's the matter?

TOOTS

I've got to go again. You forgot the pot.

MAY

The pot! How could I bring the pot? You'll have to go
yourself. That's one thing I can't do for you.

Toots gets out of bed. May helps, supporting and pushing.

TOOTS

Where is it?

MAY

Go on! Give me a minute's peace!

INT. BOBBY AND HELEN'S HALL. NIGHT

*The small figure of Toots at the end of the corridor as he makes his
slow, painful way along, holding up his pyjama bottoms.*

*Bobby, with a child in his arms, comes out of his bedroom and sees his
father.*

BOBBY

Are you okay, Dad?

TOOTS

I've got pains.

BOBBY

Now? You mean now? In your chest?

TOOTS

May!

BOBBY

Mother, Mother!

24

INT. BOBBY AND HELEN'S SPARE ROOM. NIGHT

May's anxious face as she hears their voices.

> BOBBY

Mum! Mum!

A montage of children's and adult voices from the past, shouting for her, getting louder and louder until we cut.

INT. HOSPITAL. NIGHT

Later that night. Toots lies dead on the bed.

May sits beside him on a chair. Paula and Bobby stand there.

> PAULA

Mum –

> MAY

We can't just leave. What about him?

Fade to black.

INT./EXT. CAR. DAY

Bobby drives May through a distant suburb.

> BOBBY

Shit. Which way is it?

INT./EXT. SUBURBAN HOUSE. DAY

Bobby has got May home at last. He helps her out of the car, carrying her bag.

> MAY

It doesn't feel right.

> BOBBY

It's your home.

Now, as she comes up the path behind him, he unlocks the door and leads her into the house.

INT. SUBURBAN HOUSE HALL. DAY

> BOBBY
> (*as they go in*)
>
> Are you okay? Come on . . .

May sees Toots's slippers.

> MAY
>
> Oh, look, look – they're waiting for him!

INT. SUBURBAN HOUSE BEDROOM. DAY

Bobby is unpacking his father's suitcase.

> BOBBY
>
> Where do you want his things?

> MAY
>
> How do I know! Already, it's like a museum. Just put them back.

> BOBBY
>
> Back where?

> MAY
>
> Back! Back!

INT. SUBURBAN HOUSE. DAY

Another part of the house, a little later. May has pulled out a drawer of photographs.

> BOBBY
>
> Mum, I must . . . I've . . . you know . . .

> MAY
>
> Look at these . . .

Bobby's phone rings.

> BOBBY
>
> Excuse me.

Bobby talks business on the phone in a low voice. May looks through pictures. Bobby puts the phone away and goes to May.

Why don't you sit down, Mother. Put the TV on and I'll bring you a cup of tea.

MAY

If I sit down I'll never get up again. I'll be like all the other old girls round here and then I'll go into a home.

BOBBY

I'm sure it's a common reaction.

MAY

I'd rather –

BOBBY

Mum, you can't just wander about.

Pause.

It's such a comfortable-looking chair.

MAY

You sit in it! I'm not staying!

BOBBY

Where can you go?

MAY

I don't care.

BOBBY

What do you want me to do? Don't be difficult, Mother.

MAY

Why not?

BOBBY

Sorry?

MAY

Why shouldn't I be difficult?

EXT./INT. BOBBY AND HELEN'S HOUSE. DAY

Bobby's face as he comes back into the house, carrying suitcases. We see that May is behind him.

> HELEN
> (*on phone*)
> . . . they've got to do an extra hour and if they don't we can get other people in . . . I don't know where from!

Looking up, Helen sees Bobby and then May.

> (*into phone*) Hold on.

INT. BOBBY AND HELEN'S SPARE ROOM. DAY

Bobby helps May into the room she shared with Toots.

> BOBBY
> You know where everything is.

Pause.

> Is there anything else? If you want to sit quietly, use my study, along the hall.

Pause.

> I never get the chance to go in there.

Pause.

> You know me, I must get to a meeting.

May sits down on the bed in her coat. Bobby goes.

INT. BOBBY AND HELEN'S KITCHEN. DAY

Bobby tries to leave the house, but is intercepted by Helen. Darren, working across the room, watches.

> HELEN
> What the fuck are you playing at?

> BOBBY
> My father's died, the business is going down, you're never here and when you do bother us with your presence you're

28

on the phone, it's a fucking nightmare, Helen, for me at the moment, Jesus, Jesus, you've got to take more responsibility for what's going on, and see what's happening to me, we're not going to last long at this rate, we'll be like everyone else . . .

HELEN

What's that? What do you mean?

BOBBY

The man living one place, the woman another . . . he comes round now and again . . . Jesus.

HELEN

This is not to do with that!

BOBBY

How do people not kill each other?

INT. BOBBY AND HELEN'S SPARE ROOM. DAY

May overhears some of this as she sits there sadly, not knowing what to do.

HELEN
(*voice over*)

But you can't stand her!

BOBBY
(*voice over*)

Shhhh . . . Keep your voice down.

INT. BOBBY AND HELEN'S LIVING ROOM. DAY

BOBBY

It's just for a bit.

HELEN

Oh yeah . . .

BOBBY
(*tries to hold her*)

Come on. Let's keep this together.

May appears.

> MAY
>
> I think I'll go out for a bit, cheer myself up.

They watch her go, embarrassed.

> DARREN
> *(from the conservatory, to Helen and Bobby)*
> We'll be like that one day, no one wanting us.

> HELEN
>
> No one wants you anyway.

She goes. Darren is stung by this remark.

> BOBBY
>
> I'm sure that's not entirely true.

EXT. SHEPHERD'S BUSH GREEN. DAY

May walks alone through the park. She is appalled by a number of beggars, some of whom are drunk.

EXT. SHEPHERD'S BUSH MARKET. DAY

May wanders through the market. She looks very out-of-place amongst the halal chickens and Muslim women in full burkha. She is confused, becoming lost.

EXT. SHEPHERD'S BUSH. DAY

May becomes anxious, holds on to her handbag, and walks faster and faster. The people seem rough, noisy and threatening. She stops to ask the way.

EXT. PARK. DAY

May sits in a scruffy children's playground. She starts to cry.

INT. PAULA'S FLAT. DAY

Paula opens the door to May. Paula is anxious and distressed. She hugs her mother.

INT. PAULA'S FLAT. DAY

Paula pours tea for her mum in the front room.

> MAY
> I haven't been lost for years.

> PAULA
> You're here now, Mother, safe and sound.

> MAY
> I think I liked it, just walking . . .

> PAULA
> What are we going to do with you? I know – you could
> look after Jack sometimes. In fact, I'd love to go out this
> evening . . .

> MAY
> You're not staying in?

> PAULA
> Not if I can help it. It's impossible to get a baby-sitter who
> doesn't want to be paid the earth. If you want to, sleep in
> my bed. I'll get in with Jack later.

> MAY
> Can I? This is what I came here for. I didn't expect to do
> it without Father. Sometimes I don't know what to do
> without him ordering me about.

> PAULA
> You'll have to find out, won't you?

> MAY
> Yes.

INT. PAULA'S FLAT. EVENING

*Paula, already changed, is checking herself in the mirror, moving
quickly, getting ready, heading for the door.*

> PAULA
> Is my skirt straight?

MAY

Pull it down.

PAULA

I'm not a teenager.

MAY

You're not a woman, either.

PAULA

What are you saying?

MAY

I'll ring and say I'm staying here for a bit?

PAULA

They obviously don't want you over there.

MAY

You all wanted me enough when you were children. Who's the fancy man?

PAULA

How do you know it's a man?

MAY

When will I meet him? D'you like him, Paula? What does he do?

PAULA

Shush, Mother.

MAY

Enjoy yourself, dear.

PAULA

He and I will be like a real couple tonight. (*Kisses her.*) Thanks, Mum.

INT. PAULA'S BEDROOM. NIGHT

Later. May lying in Paula's bed. The door opens and the boy Jack comes in. He slips into bed with her. She strokes the boy.

JACK
Where's Mummy? I want Mummy to cuddle me. Mummy . . .

MAY
(*sings to him*)
'Catch a falling star and put it in your pocket
Never let it fade away . . .'

INT. PAULA'S BEDROOM. NIGHT

May comes round and sits up, hearing Paula and a man talking, laughing, and banging around.

There's music and the sound of bottles opening, glasses clinking.

May starts to get out of bed.

Then Paula and the man start to make loud and vigorous love in the living room. May attempts to pile pillows round the boy's head, while stroking him. At the same time she's interested to find out what's going on.

JACK
(*half-asleep*)
Mummy . . .

MAY
It's all right, all right.

She holds him until he's quiet. Then she gets up and moves towards the door.

INT. PAULA'S LIVING ROOM. NIGHT

Looking through the door into the darkened room, May sees Paula, half-naked and distraught, and the man getting into his clothes, arguing in whispers. It is Darren.

Darren is trying to leave. Paula clings to him. They have been sharing a joint, which Darren desperately sucks at.

DARREN
Didn't we have a lovely evening? Now your mum's here, we can go out all the time. She's useful.

PAULA

But stay. Stay with me! I want to sleep in your arms! Why are men always leaving? Am I so terrible?

DARREN

I can't. The missus keeps saying it, over and over, she'll top herself. Jesus.

PAULA

Good, good! You don't even sleep with her – or do you?

DARREN

No! I wouldn't touch her! But she likes to know I'm there at least.

PAULA

Darren, my father died.

DARREN

I know, I know, sweet angel baby.

Pause.

Give me time! Your face looks so sweet when you –

PAULA

Time, time! We'll be retiring soon!

Pause.

You care for me, don't you? You still love me, don't you?

DARREN

Yes, yes . . . you know that . . . and you know I'm working on everything –

In fury she pushes him. Drunk, he falls backwards, crashing into a plant.

I'm out of here.

PAULA

Sorry, sorry. Darren. Please. I didn't mean it. Wait –

INT. PAULA'S BEDROOM. NIGHT

We watch May at the door watching Paula watching Darren leave.

34

INT./EXT. PAULA'S BEDROOM. NIGHT

The front door bangs. May goes to the window of the room and pulls the curtain aside.

She sees Darren outside, going to his van, under a street light. He leans against the van, doing up his shirt buttons, drinking from a bottle, and rubbing his bruises.

Darren looks up, sees May and smiles.

                              MAY
                            (*softly*)
        Leave her alone, you blasted brute!

May pulls the curtain. When she looks again, he's pissing against the wall. Then he slowly gets into his van.

INT. PAULA'S LIVING ROOM. NIGHT

The door opens and May appears.

She goes to Paula who lies, half-drunk and tear-stained, on the sofa in the living room. May covers her up and kisses her.

                              PAULA
        Mummy –

                              MAY
        I'm here.

EXT. MILLENNIUM BRIDGE. DAY

May on the Millennium Bridge. She looks up at the Tate Modern.

INT./EXT. TATE MODERN. DAY

May sits, sipping coffee in the canteen.

INT. TATE MODERN. DAY

May in the vast turbine hall. There is a golden statue of a young man.

EXT. BRITISH MUSEUM. DAY

May walks through the colonnades, taking her time and enjoying herself, studying the people she sees.

INT. BRITISH MUSEUM. DAY

May walks around the vast white interior.

INT. BRITISH MUSEUM RESTAURANT. DAY

May having lunch all on her own.

EXT. LONDON EYE. DAY

May surveys London from a pod on the London Eye.

INT. PAULA'S FLAT. EVENING

May is cleaning with Jack helping her.

May is now cooking and talking to Jack.

JACK

Are you very old?

MAY

Quite old. Not that old –

JACK

Will you die soon, like Grandad? People can't hear or see
when they're dead, you know.

MAY

Is that right? I like to be with your grandad but it's not my
time yet.

JACK
(*cooking*)

Shall I put them in?

MAY

Yes, go on. Good boy.

JACK

I don't mind being with you, Grandma. Will you tell me
a story? Darren tells me stories.

MAY

Does he? D'you like him?

JACK

He told me this one about the monster with bogies hanging
out of his nose. There were carrots and onions and toast
tied on and he'd go to starving people and dangle his face
down at them and –

Paula bursts through the door, home from work.

PAULA

Sorry I'm late.

JACK

She's been to her . . . therapist. Is that you how say it?

37

MAY
(*to Jack*)
Let's lay the table. Put those over there.

PAULA
This is nice.

MAY
Look!

May opens the cupboards to show how clean they are.

The filth in there!

PAULA
Thank you, Mother.

MAY
Therapist?

PAULA
(*embarrassed*)
Yes.

INT. PAULA'S KITCHEN. EVENING

They have finished eating. We can hear Jack watching TV in the next room.

PAULA
I'd like to write now. Every night I want to get started on another story. But I'm exhausted.

MAY
After last night?

PAULA
What? Oh yes. You woke up, didn't you?

MAY
You don't remember?

Pause. They look at one another. May, about to speak, restrains herself.

38

INT. PAULA'S LIVING ROOM. NIGHT

Later that night. Paula sits down opposite May.

> PAULA
> This is what it was always like.

May smiles.

> You watching TV and me trying to have a conversation.
> Now I talk to the therapist about my life.

> MAY
> Can't you talk to your hairdresser like everyone else?
> Is there something wrong with you?

> PAULA
> Yes. I've got nothing.

May laughs at the TV.

> I've been wanting to say this. I like honesty and things out
> in the open now. (*She takes a breath.*) You hardly touched
> me. You never praised or encouraged me. You didn't help
> me with my homework. You didn't think I could achieve
> anything. I never felt valued . . . That's why I'm doing it
> with a married man on the floor . . .

> MAY
> You can do better than that, and you don't have to be
> vulgar. Oh Lord, I think I'm getting a migraine.

> PAULA
> I just . . . wish I'd had all that you did. With your
> advantages I wouldn't have complained, oh no.

> MAY
> Advantages? What advantages did I have? Me?

> PAULA
> A nice house. A decent husband and a job. Two children at
> school. I could have written, seen friends, learned languages.
> What did you do? Sit on your backside watching television
> for years!

MAY

Did this woman tell you to say this? Let me meet her! Can't I have my say?

PAULA

Don't you even think I have my own bloody mind?

MAY

Paula, this is too much!

PAULA

You have to live with the consequences of what you've created, don't you understand that?

MAY

No, I don't think I do understand that.

Pause.

Paula, what's happened to you? Has someone hurt you?

INT. PAULA'S LIVING ROOM. NIGHT

May, unable to sleep, distressed.

INT. PAULA'S BEDROOM. NIGHT

May goes into Paula's room. Paula has fallen asleep with pen and papers scattered around. May touches her; Paula is awake.

MAY

I was unhappy.

PAULA

All my life?

MAY

I've never been strong. It's all been too much for me.

PAULA

Let's forget you for a second. What about me and what I'm left with?

MAY

You're healthy. You're intelligent –

40

PAULA

I want him to be with me.

MAY

Who? That man? The builder? He's rough, with no
qualifications, or money, or –

PAULA

That's what I want.

MAY

You can do better than him!

PAULA

I will make it happen, you'll see, if you help me for once.

MAY

What can I do?

PAULA

I love him!

MAY

Him! You don't! Why?

PAULA

He's my only chance. He doesn't really live with his wife.
He sleeps in a van outside the house.

MAY

He does?

PAULA

He won't leave because of his son. He has an autistic son
he adores. Darren's a good man, just a little crazy . . . like
a lot of people.

MAY

What d'you mean?

PAULA

If you'd only help me get on, Mother. You might as well be
of use to others now.

MAY

Is that what you think?

Pause.

> Okay, I'll help you. Let's see what we can do for one
> another. I'll help you.

EXT. SCHOOL GATES. DAY

May collects Jack from school.

INT. BOBBY AND HELEN'S KITCHEN. DAY

*May potters around making Jack's tea, glancing now and then at
Darren working in the conservatory.*

She fetches a chair where she sits chopping vegetables, watching Darren.

*When he glances up at her, she leans back quickly. When she looks
again, he has gone.*

Suddenly, behind her, Jack bursts through the door, startling her.

JACK

Is it ready?

MAY

What? No, not quite yet.

JACK

I'm starving!

Darren comes in with some chocolate for Jack.

DARREN

Here we go!

JACK

Chocolate!

*Jack rushes out. In the background we can hear a kid's TV programme
being switched on.*

DARREN

Hello. (*Puts out his hand.*) I've seen you, of course, but we
haven't met properly. Darren. I talked to your husband for
a minute. I'm sorry.

MAY

Yes, thank you.

DARREN

I've got to go and pick up my own boy. My wife's gone to
see her sister.

MAY

You're married?

DARREN

For longer than I can remember. Not that I can remember
anything now. Er . . . who am I?

MAY

What are you doing with Paula?

DARREN

Listening to her, mostly. I've got good ears.

MAY

Do you care for and about her?

DARREN

How can you ask that?

Pause.

How can you?

INT. BOBBY AND HELEN'S KITCHEN. DAY

*May and Darren are having tea together. Darren takes a bottle
of brandy from a cupboard and offers some to May.*

MAY

No . . . no thank you . . .

Darren pours a slug into his mug of tea.

DARREN

A little bit of what you fancy does you good.

She watches him drink.

43

MAY

Do you ever work for anyone else?

DARREN

If I can't help it.

MAY

I worked in shops for years. Shoe shops.

DARREN

Really? Everybody needs shoes. A few pairs, at least. There
aren't many people without shoes. What else do people
have to have? If you could work that out, you could make
a lot of money.

MAY

What do you think?

DARREN

I don't know! Love! That's why I'm not rich!

MAY

I would like to show you these.

*He is looking at the photographs she has laid on the table. There's a
picture of the house, and Bobby, Paula and Toots standing in front of
it years ago.*

DARREN

I found something the other day, in one of my father's old
jackets. It was a shopping list my mother had written for
him . . . in her own hand of course. And it became the most
valuable thing I'd ever touched. It's odd . . . I think all the
time now – and I wish I didn't – of what remains of us
when we're gone.

MAY

I can't go back home. I don't know what I'm doing. I'm
frightened.

DARREN

Are you?

Pause.

You imagine people getting less frightened as they get older. You think they'll come to terms with things.

MAY

No. Perhaps. But yes, they do.

DARREN

Something to look forward to.

Jack come in.

JACK

Darren, I want to be the centre of attention.

DARREN

But so do I!

JACK

How do snails stick, then?

DARREN

Same way people stick to the earth, I guess. With glue on the bottom of their feet. Haven't you got glue on your shoes?

INT. BOBBY AND HELEN'S HALL. DAY

Paula comes in, carrying newspapers, notebooks, the Harry Potter omnibus, and her school bag.

INT. BOBBY AND HELEN'S KITCHEN. DAY

Paula comes in and finds May, Darren and Jack sitting together. Darren is reading aloud. Paula stands and watches a moment.

DARREN

'Beware the Jabberwock, my son!
The jaws that bite, the claws that catch!
He took his . . .'

Pause.

He didn't took his anything.

PAULA

What a happy family!

JACK

Bandersnatch! Bandersnatch!

PAULA

Yes, dear.

Darren gets up.

DARREN
(*to May*)

Lovely to talk to you.

MAY

Yes.

INT. BOBBY AND HELEN'S HOUSE. DAY

May clears away the tea things. As she does so, she can see Paula and Darren in the conservatory. Darren is packing up for the day.

PAULA

I've written something . . . I want to read it to you, and you say what you think, like we did before . . .

DARREN

Tomorrow . . . I'll try and come by.

PAULA

I'll buy us a house. I think I'm getting somewhere.

DARREN

How?

PAULA
(*she taps the Harry Potter*)

Other people can do this.

DARREN
(*pause*)

I'm going to be late for the boy. She'll kill me.

Paula kisses him.

PAULA

I'm getting so impatient I could kill.

May's face. She is very still.

INT. PAULA'S FLAT. NIGHT

Later that night. May sits on the sofa watching TV with Jack asleep beside her.

Paula sits at the table, drinking, trying to write.

MAY

I went to the art gallery by myself and then Bobby took me out for lunch. Very posh, he thought it was. He said, 'I can always get a table here.'

PAULA

What did you say?

MAY

'It's a restaurant, Bobby. They're supposed to have tables for people to sit and eat at.'

PAULA

He's got so pompous.

They laugh.

MAY

Does Darren take you anywhere nice?

PAULA

Like where?

MAY

Opera. Theatre. Holidays.

PAULA

We go to the pub before he goes home. What did you talk to him about at Bobby's house? Did he mention me?

MAY

He likes you.

PAULA

Oh, did he say that? Sometimes I think he'll never leave her.

MAY

Why's he so marvellous, this man?

PAULA

Your snobbery stops you seeing anything positive about him. He's clever, sweet, generous. talented . . . He's very, very weak, too.

Pause.

I'll get up early tomorrow and write then. In two or three years I'll be able to support us properly. I'm going to have a child with him before it's too late.

MAY

Does he want that?

PAULA

He will.

MAY

Paula, I wanted to say, if you haven't got anywhere with the writing yet – and with one or two other things – perhaps it would be better to do something that will lead to –

PAULA

Believe, believe, old woman! Just once – believe in me! Say something that makes me feel better!

MAY

Don't be so harsh with me, Paula!

PAULA

I am harsh. Yes. Because I think you're right.

MAY
(*surprised*)

What?

PAULA

That's why I'm upset. Listen, forget what I said. I am going to finish with that bastard and get liberated! He's been lowering my self-esteem for months.

MAY

You will have to rid yourself of false hope in the end.

PAULA

False hope? I'd better make the end sooner rather than later.
I've been thinking of leaving him from the moment I met
him. I'll tell him tomorrow. Why shouldn't I do it? I'll
suffer, then I'll be free. Okay! Thank you . . . for giving me
the courage. I'm going to make a new start, without him.

Pause.

Then we'll see him fall apart, the bastard.

EXT. LONDON STREET. DAY

May sits outside a delicatessen, drinking coffee and eating croissants.

She is reading Time Out *for the first time, marking things, trying to
figure it out, changing her glasses.*

The deli owner comes over.

OWNER

Finished?

MAY

I'll take a croissant for a friend, I think.

INT. BOBBY AND HELEN'S HOUSE. MORNING

*The house is quiet. We see May walking across the living room to the
French windows holding the croissant in a little bag. She looks into the
conservatory where Darren is working.*

*Suddenly Bobby comes out, on his way somewhere else. May is
surprised to see him.*

BOBBY

Hi, Mum –

MAY

Oh God, you scared me. I've . . . I've come to listen to
some music. Will you sit with me? We hardly talked at lunch.

49

BOBBY
You didn't stop, dear. Enjoy!

INT. BOBBY AND HELEN'S HOUSE. DAY

May puts on a CD. She makes sure that music can be heard in the conservatory. She looks at Darren, who is stripped to the waist, working.

INT. BOBBY AND HELEN'S HOUSE. DAY

May fills a cafetière with boiling water. Lots of steam.

INT./EXT. BOBBY AND HELEN'S HOUSE. DAY

Darren cooks up a bucket of boiling pitch in the garden. He uses the hot pitch, which he paints on the conservatory floor, to fix the hard wood blocks.

INT. BOBBY AND HELEN'S HOUSE. DAY

May has put the croissant on a tray. Butter and jam. Coffee. She approaches him with the croissant but is nervous of disturbing him.

MAY
Darren, I brought you this.

Darren stops work. He smiles.

DARREN
Waitress service!

INT. BOBBY AND HELEN'S HOUSE. DAY

Darren eats his breakfast.

MAY
Is my daughter talented, do you think?

DARREN
I love her voice – when she reads to me.

50

MAY

You believe in her, then?

DARREN

Good luck to her with whatever she wants, I say.

MAY

It is not necessarily how she should spend her life.

DARREN

Who knows the answer to how anyone should spend their
life?

MAY

I thought . . . yesterday – now I only want to do interesting
things . . . things I love . . .

DARREN
(*going back to work*)
Helen will think I'm slacking.

MAY

She's very . . .

DARREN

She certainly is. Very, very. She's jealous of you, of everyone –
that's all.

MAY

How do you deal with her?

DARREN
(*laughs*)
I tell her she looks like Jean Shrimpton.

MAY

Every day?

DARREN

It has a calming effect on most women, I find.

She says something under her breath.

Sorry?

MAY

I said, dear God, let us be alive before we die.

DARREN
(laughing)
Hey . . . we'll have lunch, shall we?

MAY

Shall we?

INT. BOBBY AND HELEN'S BATHROOM. DAY

May is at the mirror, looking at herself. She reaches out to touch things . . . and at last she puts on Helen's perfume.

EXT. RIVER. DAY

Darren and May are sitting on a bench at a riverside pub. Darren finishes his pint.

MAY

Give us a chance

DARREN

Get it down you, girl. I've got something to show you.

MAY
(*knocking back her drink*)

It was a double.

DARREN

At least! Good for you.

MAY

You've got a ruddy cheek.

DARREN

Come on, darlin'!

EXT. RIVER. DAY

They walk along the river.

MAY

You see, I don't believe you really want to be with my
daughter.

Pause.

You're making her frantic, not being straight.

DARREN

Nearly there.

MAY

If you want to be with her, tell me . . . then I can reassure her.

DARREN

I am with her.

EXT. RIVER. DAY

DARREN

Here –

It's a cemetery. She hesitates.

Sorry, I forgot. How stupid.

MAY

I'll be all right with you.

He takes her arm and leads her in.

EXT. CEMETERY. DAY

Darren and May stand before Hogarth's tomb.

DARREN

Hogarth. His house is round the corner but I shouldn't think he's in. Read the rhyme.

She reads the inscription.

MAY

'Farewell Great Painter of Mankind
Who Mastered the noblest form of art,
Where pictures of morals charm the mind.

'If Genius free thee, reader hear,
If Nature touch thee, drop a tear.
If neither move thee, run from here
For Hogarth's dust doth lie here.'

I had no idea it was here. I might come back and draw it later

Darren thinks for a moment, then produces a stub of pencil from a back pocket and a scrap of old paper from somewhere, which he flattens out with his palm.

DARREN

Do it now.

MAY
(smiles)

I said I'd get Paula's shopping.

DARREN

You serve others too often.

54

EXT. RIVER. DAY

They walk along the tidal reach.

> MAY
>
> I like being with you so much.

May stumbles.

> Sorry, I'm not used to drinking at lunchtime. My head's
> gone.

*She falls against him and they kiss and hold one another. She reaches
for his hands.*

> Oh God, I don't know what's happened to me.

> DARREN
>
> I think you just fell.

                              MAY
    I've got to go.

She pulls away. He watches her hurry from him.

                            DARREN
                            (*calls*)
    See you later!

INT. PAULA'S LIVING ROOM. EVENING

Paula comes in and sees May standing in front of a mirror,
surrounded by bags, trying her new clothes on. The clothes are
expensive, flowing, 'artistic' or 'bohemian'.

                             PAULA
    Very sixties.

                              MAY
    I was washing nappies at the time. By hand.

                             PAULA
    Let's eat. I've got some wine and a video for later. Unless
    you're going out with a man.

                              MAY
    That would be my lucky day!

                             PAULA
    I've been thinking . . . there's someone I've got in mind for
    you . . . at my writer's group.

                              MAY
    Oh no.

                             PAULA
    Wait and see. I think you'll enjoy it anyway.

Pause.

    I just saw Darren.

                              MAY
    Oh yes.

                              56

Pause.

> Did you tell him?

PAULA

Tell him what?

MAY

That you're leaving him.

PAULA

I kept thinking his mind was on someone else . . . The bastard likes girls too much. Not that I'd mind, to be honest.

MAY

Wouldn't you?

PAULA

Did you see him at Bobby's?

MAY

Only . . . briefly.

PAULA

Are you getting any sense out of him about what he wants to do with me?

MAY

Not yet . . .

PAULA

Once I know, I can make some serious decisions.

MAY

I feel different . . . in these clothes. A different person.

PAULA

What a relief.

INT. BOBBY AND HELEN'S CONSERVATORY/LIVING ROOM. DAY

Darren is working in the conservatory.

May, in her new clothes, comes through the living room with bowls of pasta and salad on a tray.

She takes the food to Darren, regarding him nervously. He looks at her and smiles.

INT. BOBBY AND HELEN'S HOUSE. DAY

Darren tucks in.

> MAY
>
> I spent the morning shopping. I hope you don't mind . . .
> I've brought you something.

She takes a book from a bag and gives it to him. It is a book of 'great' drawings. He looks through it.

> DARREN
>
> How kind . . . how kind you are . . .

> MAY
>
> You like it?

> DARREN
>
> It's beautiful.

> MAY
>
> Look.

She shows him Dürer's drawing of his mother.

> DARREN
> (*pause*)
> If only I'd started earlier. (*He looks at the book.*) I feel . . .

> MAY
>
> What?

> DARREN
>
> Filled up by it. And ignorant. That I don't know anything.

> MAY
>
> But that you want to know?

He goes to kiss her. She turns away. He laughs at her. She looks at him. He smiles. She smiles back.

INT. BOBBY AND HELEN'S CONSERVATORY. DAY

Later. She is drawing Darren as he works in the conservatory.

> DARREN
> I haven't got time to keep still!

> MAY
> Doesn't matter! It's years since I've done this. I love it,
> I love it. I'm talentless and I don't care!

As she draws, May talks.

> If you asked me to describe my life and what I've done, as
> you did yesterday . . . I'd say nothing much . . .

> DARREN
> No –

> MAY
> It's only that . . . a family, a house, a marriage . . . they
> would be enough, and difficult enough for a whole life.
> I wouldn't underestimate it. Except I wasn't there . . . I was
> too critical of myself, too hard on myself . . . it's been a
> waste of time . . . I was too worried about everything to live
> in it properly.

May lights a cigarette. Darren is surprised.

> I was a terrible housewife. But that's what all the women
> did then. We aren't like Helen and Paula. I just went along
> with it . . . until . . .

> DARREN
> Until?

> MAY
> Until a few minutes ago, actually.

> DARREN
> Looks like we've got a rebel on our hands.

> MAY
> A few years ago, an intelligent man who lived nearby, an
> antique dealer, started to like me. Twice he took me into his
> bed.

DARREN

Did you like it?

MAY

Lord, yes. I planned to go away with him. I would go to
my husband and explain. But I never saw the man again.
I couldn't upset anyone.

Pause.

Oh, Darren, the cigarette's made my chest all congested –
I can't breathe!

DARREN

If you do breathe, what will happen?

MAY

I'd say . . . would it be a trouble if . . . would you mind . . .
The spare room's . . . Would you come to the spare room
with me?

Pause.

Would you?

INT. BOBBY AND HELEN'S HALL. DAY

*She leads the way to the spare room, and turns to watch him following
her. She hesitates. Stands still, bows her head.*

He takes her arm and leads her into the room.

INT. BOBBY AND HELEN'S SPARE ROOM. DAY

May sits there in bra and pants. He looks at her.

MAY

What do you see? A shapeless old lump.

He starts to hum an aria from Don Giovanni *and she smiles.*

Come . . . Can I do something to you? Would you mind?
I feel such a passion . . . I should have been doing this . . .
before . . .

DARREN

You want to touch me? You can touch me.

MAY

Will you touch me?

DARREN

If you let me.

MAY

Oh, I want it. But why? Why?

She puts her face to his stomach.

DARREN

You're lonely.

MAY

What's that to you?

DARREN

I don't know.

62

INT. BOBBY AND HELEN'S SPARE ROOM. DAY

They are in bed. He touches her.

> MAY
>
> I thought, the other day, no one will ever touch me again, apart from the undertaker.

He touches her.

INT. HELEN'S BATHROOM. LATE AFTERNOON

May washes her face in the basin.

As her head comes up into the mirror, she looks at her own face. Darren stands in the doorway behind her.

> MAY
>
> I'm hot, I'm so hot, I think I'm burning up.

INT. PAULA'S FLAT. EVENING

May, sleeves rolled up, is washing the floor. Paula comes in.

> MAY
>
> Just getting things in ship-shape.

> PAULA
>
> I'm so glad you've perked up, Mother.

> MAY
>
> Is it all right if I take the curtains down?

> PAULA
>
> Sure.

May looks at Paula as she unpacks her work bag, singing to herself.

> MAY
>
> I heard this record today . . . at Bobby's. It went, 'I ain't good-looking, babe, and I don't dress fine, but I'm a travelling woman with a travelling mind!'

She laughs a little hysterically.

PAULA

Calm down, Mother. Is it because you miss Dad?

MAY

No. I like the song.

PAULA

You never travel anywhere, darling.

INT. PAULA'S KITCHEN AND LIVING ROOM. EVENING

Later. May is laying the table for supper.

PAULA

Can you lay an extra place? (*Ensuring Jack can't overhear,
Paula goes to her.*) What has he been saying?

MAY

Who?

PAULA

You know who.

MAY

But you've left him, surely?

PAULA

Why do you keep saying that, repeating yourself like
a wretched parrot! When the time's right, I will. Now –

MAY
(*going into the other room*)
I didn't really get the chance to go into things –

PAULA

You had lunch.

MAY

Yes, we did –

PAULA

He took you out – he told me. And?

MAY

I couldn't just plunge in. It'll take time. It's a long game –
don't they say that?

PAULA

My life depends on it, Mother. Jack keeps asking when
Darren and I will be together. He can't wait. I've got to
give him some stability. He's never really had a father.

MAY

Oh Paula, is he the best choice?

Pause.

What would you do if I weren't here?

PAULA

It's your chance now, Mother, to help me.

MAY

With men you have to . . . you have to draw them in . . .
coax, negotiate . . . they're like frightened birds . . . If you
say boo, they'll flee.

PAULA

You're the expert now, are you?

Darren comes to the window behind them and watches them bicker.

MAY

I do know some things –

PAULA

If you really did, you'd have done more –

MAY

All right, all right, don't pull me to pieces –

PAULA

That's a bit rich –

*Darren knocks on the window and waves. Paula jumps up and opens
the door.*

DARREN

Ladies, ladies, please.

PAULA

Hi, cowboy!

May watches as Paula kisses him in the hallway.

DARREN

Evening, May.

INT. PAULA'S KITCHEN. EVENING

Darren and May sit opposite one another at the table, sipping wine.

Paula talks as she cooks and serves the couple.

PAULA

Everyone has their story, I guess. They want to put their
side of things. I want to . . . without that they go mad.
It's self-expression and therapy I'm interested in. If I could
find a way of doing that with the children at school, I'd
be uniting various things . . . I could write about that . . .
a sort of textbook . . . that's something I could usefully
do . . .

INT. PAULA'S LIVING ROOM. EVENING

*Later. Darren sits with Paula on the sofa. He is reading one of her
manuscripts. May, clearing the table, looks over.*

DARREN

This is good.

PAULA

Is it?

DARREN

It's the best thing so far. You should read it to the group.

*Paula looks across at May and nods in confirmation. Paula kisses
Darren.*

PAULA

Time for bed I think, Mother, don't you?

MAY

Yes, sorry. Of course. Actually, I'll go out.

PAULA

At this time?

MAY

It's all right. I'm not afraid now. Not afraid of anything.
(*Sings.*) 'I'm a travelling woman with a . . .'

DARREN

(*he watches May go. To Paula*)

Where's she going?

PAULA

It's not your problem. She's starting to get on my nerves.
I'll talk to Bobby about sending her home. I'm getting sick
of taking all the responsibility.

Pause.

Will you read my piece again?

DARREN

Again?

Pause.

Sure.

May goes out of the front door.

EXT. BAR. NIGHT

*May sits alone in a rather louche bar, with much younger people,
nursing her drink and clearly relishing her thoughts. Her pleasure is in
being alone as she thinks of her new 'lover'.*

BARMAN

You all right there?

May looks past him at her reflection on the mirror behind the bar.

MAY

Hmmmm?

EXT. PAULA'S STREET. NIGHT

From across the road, May watches Paula say goodnight to Darren and close the door. Darren comes out and gets into his van. May comes out of the shadows and wants to go to him, but holds back. He is gone before she reaches him. She watches the van drive away.

INT. PAULA'S FLAT. NIGHT

May comes into the flat. Paula, tousled, in her dressing gown, is picking up her clothes from the floor.

> PAULA
>
> That's cheered me up.

EXT. CAFÉ. DAY

May sits outside. In front of her, a cappuccino sits untouched. She thinks.

INT. BOBBY AND HELEN'S HOUSE. CONSERVATORY. DAY

Darren is working. It feels very hot in the conservatory. May comes in. She looks at him. She says nothing.

> DARREN
>
> What's for lunch?

> MAY
>
> I don't want any lunch.

Darren looks at May. He says nothing. She kisses him. He responds. They smile at one another. May touches him.

> Take me upstairs.

The front door slams, Bobby comes in. For a moment he looks at them. May moves away from Darren.

> BOBBY
>
> I never have any time and now I have I don't know what to do with myself.

DARREN

Christ, Bobby. Come and have a smoke, it's been non-stop.

BOBBY

Yeah, let's do that. Then I've promised to see Paula.

MAY

What about?

BOBBY

She'll be asking for something, I'd imagine.

MAY

Is your work going to be all right?

BOBBY

I don't know. I just don't know.

Pause.

I wondered if you'd go round to the supermarket and get some food in. You know where it is by now, don't you?

When she's gone, he looks at Darren.

All you do when you've got money is pay people to do what your mother did for free when you were a kid.

INT. BOBBY AND HELEN'S HOUSE. DAY

May, in her coat, preparing to leave, watches Darren and Bobby sitting in the conservatory, smoking dope and laughing, whilst listening to loud music.

BOBBY

You're lucky.

DARREN

Why?

BOBBY

You work with your hands. It's steady. You don't have to spend all day watching the exchange rate go up and down and having breakfast with your lawyers.

                              DARREN
You'll never be poor.

                              BOBBY
I don't deserve to be fucking poor.

INT. SUPERMARKET. DAY

May is in the supermarket, looking at food she doesn't understand: squash, sun-dried tomatoes, scores of cheeses. The supermarket is filled with women of her age or older. She looks at all the other grannies as if for the first time.

INT. BOBBY AND HELEN'S HOUSE. DAY

Paula comes in and finds Bobby and Darren talking.

                              PAULA
Guys –

                              DARREN
Wanna smoke?

                              PAULA
                            (*to Bobby*)
Can I have a word?

INT. BOBBY AND HELEN'S HOUSE. DAY

Paula follows Bobby into the lounge.

                              PAULA
What's he been saying?

                              BOBBY
I dunno. At least it's coming along a bit faster now.

                              PAULA
I mean about me, not the fucking floor.

                              BOBBY
How should I know? I'm not the fucking go-between! How can I show the house to buyers with the conservatory half-

finished and him standing there with his arse hanging out
of his trousers?

PAULA

You're selling? You're selling the house already? Are you
crazy?

BOBBY

I don't have any choice. (*Beat.*) That wretched cardigan
shop is haemorrhaging all my fucking money. Of course
it had to be on the poshest bit of the fucking Portobello
Road. And of course she fucking insisted on opening it
at precisely the worst possible moment for me.

PAULA

I thought you were loaded.

BOBBY

So did I. Nobody wants what I've got to offer any more.

PAULA

Poor little brother.

BOBBY

Aren't you pleased? You've always been bloody envious of
me, but I can tell you, you wouldn't be envious of my state
of mind at the moment.

*During this he accidentally knocks May's capacious bag, which falls
over on the table. Everything falls out. There are art magazines and
art books, and a folder of May's work.*

Shit.

*Paula looks at May's art folder: drawings of a man naked. It could
be Darren. There is one erotic picture, of a woman sucking a man's
penis.*

PAULA

Have you actually looked at these?

BOBBY

Eh?

> PAULA

Look. She's having him.

> BOBBY

Who?

> PAULA

Mum. Mother. May.

> BOBBY

You're ridiculous.

> PAULA

Get up off your lazy arse for once!

Bobby comes and looks over her shoulder at the sketches.

> BOBBY

Christ, I feel as if I've just had a very hot curry.

Paula turns a page in the sketch book.

Fucking hell! The old slapper! It's fantasy. She wouldn't do that. Would she?

They both look across at Darren, working away in the conservatory, unawares, stripped to the waist.

If it's true, your boyfriend's even more of a fuck-up than I thought.

Paula shakes her head in disbelief. Her eyes sparkle with tears.

If she's been stupid . . . don't hurt her.

> PAULA

Hurt her? Hurt her? You idiot!

Paula rushes out. Bobby looks at Darren.

INT. BOBBY AND HELEN'S KITCHEN. DAY

Bobby is drinking a beer and thinking. Darren comes in.

> DARREN

I'm off, then.

Pause. Bobby looks at him.

Everything all right, mate?

> BOBBY

Yeah.

Bobby looks at him.

> DARREN

What?

> BOBBY

Nothing.

> DARREN

Fancy a pint?

> BOBBY

I'm a bit busy.

> DARREN

Right. I'm off.

INT. PAULA'S FLAT. EVENING

Paula has changed. May is also ready to go out, wearing the clothes she has bought recently.

> MAY

Is this all right?

Paula is looking hard at May, very controlled but severe.

Who are the people we're going to see?

> PAULA

I've told you. They're writers of different ability.

> MAY
> (*Paula is looking at her*)

Am I okay?

> PAULA

Mother?

                          MAY
What?

                          PAULA
No, nothing . . . nothing.

INT. CHURCH HALL. EVENING

Fifteen writers are gathered in the church hall, ready to start. They talk, make tea, prepare their stationery, etc. The writers are different ages and types: a road-sweeper, a doctor, students, pensioners. Paula makes tea for May.

                          PAULA
We've been working together for over a year. Some of them have really come on. Their lives have changed and –

                          MAY
How?

                          PAULA
I don't know, they've moved house, changed jobs, fallen in love with the right people for a change . . .

                           74

INT. CHURCH HALL. EVENING

The writers sit in a circle. One of them, a man in his sixties, reading.

> **BRUCE**
> One night, after two and a half years together, his wife refused him. Something atrocious had happened between them. They never made love again, not once, their faces looking at opposite walls for years, until she died. And he realised that he had wasted his time, and wasted hers . . . and that he was bitter . . . and wanted . . . wanted . . .

Pause.

The group looks at Paula.

> **PAULA**
> Let's carry on with this good work. A story of childhood now . . . of what it was like then, an accurate, precisely drawn picture.

We see them all thinking and starting to make notes.

> Find a quiet place then . . .

INT. CHURCH HALL. EVENING

The group has broken up. With pens, pencils and pads, they sit on chairs, on the floor – one of them lies on a table – to write. May looks around anxiously.

> **PAULA**
> You don't have to do this,. Mum.

> **MAY**
> No, I will, now I'm here. Why not?

She looks across the room, where she sees, on a table, big sheets of paper and crayons.

INT. CHURCH HALL. EVENING

May is on her knees on the floor, writing and drawing on the big sheets of paper.

Bruce comes up behind her. Paula is watching from close by.

BRUCE

That's great, that is.

MAY

A memory from forty years ago – with words. A catastrophe, eh?

PAULA

Read it out, Mum. Go on. Everyone here does it.

OTHERS

Yes, yes.

INT. CHURCH HALL. EVENING

May is reading. The audience is quiet.

MAY

I'd put the children to bed at last. It was such a struggle. I'd hate them by the end of the day and thought I was the only parent who felt that way. They'd be screaming upstairs, throwing things out of their cots. I'd put on my coat and shut the front door behind me . . . I'd go out, and walk across the fields for miles, as I do now. Or I'd go to a pub where no one knew me. I made sure I'd be back before my husband. But they'd be asleep at last. I wanted to kill myself out of guilt. I still haven't recovered from those cries . . . what is it about those cries . . . ?

INT. CHURCH HALL. EVENING

She has finished reading. People are congratulating her. We see Paula pushing Bruce towards May again.

BRUCE

May. I'm Bruce, by the way. Would you like to come out with some of us, tonight? I really liked what you did. It was . . . gutsy . . .

MAY

It's a little too late for me now, I'm afraid, I get tired.
(*She looks at Paula.*) I enjoyed that. I didn't know such –
workshops, as you call them, even existed. I could go all
the time.

PAULA

Why don't you go out with Bruce, Mother?

MAY

I will then. Not now, but another night.

BRUCE

I'd like that very much.

INT. PAULA'S LIVING ROOM. NIGHT

Paula has made up a bed on the sofa for May.

PAULA

It's the sofa tonight, Mother, I'm afraid. I hope you don't
have any nightmares. I'm glad you liked Bruce. He's a
widower with a lot of money. But maybe it's too soon –
you just wouldn't be interested in anyone else.

MAY

No, no, not now, not ever again.

PAULA

And certainly not so soon after Dad. But you could have
a friendship, at least. I'll arrange something with Bruce
anyway – he's not too old for you, is he? You wouldn't
prefer –

MAY

That thing he wrote was rather upsetting, wasn't it? What
a lonely man. They all seemed a bit odd, though. And
everyone was so sycophantic about each others' work.

PAULA

Did they? Shall I tell you why it seems like that, Mother?
What they want, for once in their life, is to be properly
listened to, to be heard.

77

MAY
(*pause*)
You're very kind. I'm sorry, I didn't see that at the time.

PAULA
No, well.

Pause.

I miss my darling Darren tonight.

MAY
He's got a story, too. Didn't he have a wretched time as a young man?

PAULA
Is that right?

MAY
I think people hurt him a lot.

PAULA
He told you, did he? What else did he say? Come on, tell me. You've got to. That's what I asked you to do.

MAY
Don't ask me.

Pause.

I don't know him.

PAULA
What does he say about me? You've brought it up, haven't you? Come on!

MAY
But you'd be a fool to spend your whole life beating your head against a wall. Open your eyes, dear, and see what else is out there.

PAULA
Perhaps I should.

INT. PAULA'S FLAT. NIGHT

May, from her sofa-bed, watches Paula sitting there thinking.

MAY

Paula, d'you think this therapy is helping you?

PAULA

I want us all to go out together.

MAY

When? I don't know if I –

PAULA

What are you doing tomorrow?

INT. BOBBY AND HELEN'S SPARE ROOM. DAY

We hear May's cries before we see her.

Darren is fucking May slowly. She lies there enjoying it. He holds her when she comes.

DARREN

There, there, there, there . . .

INT. BOBBY AND HELEN'S SPARE ROOM. DAY

Now Darren is sitting up and she massages his back. The window is open. The wind blows the curtains.

MAY

Up you get.

DARREN

Oh, I don't think I can do it again.

She laughs. Darren takes a handful of pills, washes them down with a gulp from a bottle of wine.

MAY

What are they?

DARREN

Dunno. Found them in Helen's bathroom.

MAY

Would you take anything?

DARREN

Always have.

MAY

Why's that?

DARREN

Dunno . . .

Pause.

I love these afternoons. The peace . . .

Pause.

My boy Arlo is the sweetest, most beautiful mad creature . . .
And there's Paula . . . you ask about her, but I'm only
bluffing. Since the boy was born I haven't had a day to
think about who I am, or what I should do . . .

MAY

How could you? What do you want, darling? Tell Mother.

DARREN

Six months away. You know, go through in my mind, repair
myself.

MAY

Why can't you?

DARREN

Me, I work, but I save nothing. There's pubs I can't go into,
the people are looking for me.

MAY

I'll pay for you. To travel and live.

DARREN

Why would you do that?

MAY

I want to. We'll go away.

Pause.

Oh, it's a stupid idea. Don't you feel terrible about this?

DARREN

I never care about what other people think. What difference does it make? I always end up in trouble anyway.

MAY

I've never had enough trouble. My husband liked me being at home not doing much. I was to look after him. He hated me having friends, so I didn't have any.

DARREN

Why did you do what he said?

MAY

What? I wanted him to be happy. We didn't really have that feminism then, you know.

DARREN

I guess some men like depressed women.

MAY

What? What did you say?

DARREN

It suits some men to have their women unhappy. Bobby's like that.

MAY

They keep the women that way, is that what you're saying? But I never thought about that. Lord, the things you need to know. They just don't occur to you!

He lets her think for a bit.

DARREN

Paula told me on the phone this morning that you have an admirer.

MAY

The old girl's suddenly in demand! Would you mind?

DARREN

You won't like anyone more than me.

MAY

Why's that?

DARREN

You know.

MAY

No. But we'll see . . . won't we?

DARREN

You old tart.

INT. BOBBY AND HELEN'S SPARE ROOM. DAY

She lies there, watching Darren get into his shirt, shorts, trousers, admiring his body.

DARREN

Did you mean what you said?

MAY

I wouldn't want to leave them anything. You're the only one who's been nice to me up here.

EXT. PUB. DAY

Darren, Bruce, May and Paula have gone to a pub beside the river, where they sit outside.

DARREN
(getting up)

I'll get them in.

He stands beside Paula, patting his pockets, nodding at May. Automatically Paula gives him money.

MAY
(follows him)

I'll give you a hand.

82

Paula watches them go into the pub while Bruce talks in her ear, somewhat relentlessly.

                    BRUCE
My writing's really started to develop . . . those exercises
you gave us . . . and your insistence on us working every
day were really useful . . . I'm getting the discipline at
last . . .

                    PAULA
Mine's gone. Everything's gone.

INT. PUB. DAY

At the bar, Darren orders the drinks. The barmaid is a girl of twenty.

                    GIRL
And what does your mother want?

DARREN

Mother? We'll have a couple of whisky macs, don't you think, May?

GIRL

What are they, then?

Darren begins to explain.

She leans across to him. Darren goes into a charming explanation of the nature of whisky macs, brandy macs and their sobriquets.

EXT. PUB. DAY

May comes out of the pub with drinks for Paula and Bruce.

PAULA

Everything all right, Mum? You look a little pale.

MAY

This is lovely.

INT. PUB. DAY

May returns to the bar. Darren is still talking to the barmaid. They take their drinks.

MAY

What are you playing at?

DARREN

I like other people. (*Lowers his voice.*) I can still smell you on me.

As they walk to the door.

MAY

She's watching us like a hawk.

EXT. PUB. DAY

They're all eating supper, apart from Darren, who just drinks quickly and is restless and agitated. Paula watches Darren and May together.

PAULA

Eat something, Darren.

He shakes his head.

Don't you think he should, Mother?

MAY

He's a big lad.

Silence.

BRUCE
(*to May*)
Will you come to other meetings of the group? You're an
extraordinary talent – you have a necessary wildness –

MAY

If Paula lets me. I don't know how long I can impose
myself on her up here in London.

BRUCE

We can find you another place to stay if you don't want
to go back.

PAULA

What an excellent offer!

Paula sees Darren is looking away, downriver.

So when are you going to get around to finishing my study?

DARREN

I haven't finished the conservatory.

PAULA

Oh, I wouldn't bother with that. They're selling up.

Darren looks up.

What, you didn't know?

DARREN

I can't believe he'd not tell me.

PAULA

There's a lot of things people don't tell one another. The
work you've done on the house will make them even richer.

(*to Bruce*). Darren and I are getting a place further out –
this year.

BRUCE

Lovely.

MAY

(*to Darren, who's shaking his head*)
What's wrong?

DARREN

Why does he do that? I haven't been working for months
on end so he can just sell up. Why does he do that?

*Darren gets up and goes to the rail overlooking the river. He overhangs
the side. May wants so much to go to him. Paula watches her.*

BRUCE

(*to May*)
What are we going to do, miss? I feel all lively.

PAULA

I'm so glad you two like one another.

EXT. RIVERSIDE. EVENING

Paula is holding on to Darren as they walk along.

BRUCE

(*to May*)
Lucky Darren's going back with his Paula later. Why don't
you come and see my books?

PAULA

What a lovely invitation! Why don't you do that, Mum?
We'll see you later.

MAY

Wait . . . please . . . can't we . . . let's go somewhere else
first.

BRUCE

You like a drink, eh? I've got the car. Come on, everyone!

He strides off.

> MAY
> I know what you're trying to do.

> PAULA
> Come on, Mother, let's have some fun.

INT. CAR/EXT. STREET. NIGHT

Bruce has parked the car. Paula and Darren have got out, leaving Bruce and May.

As May is about to get out, Bruce halts her.

> BRUCE
> I like you.

He tries to kiss her. She pulls away. At last she tries to respond. We see that Paula has been watching. She nudges Darren.

> PAULA
> Look. Look! Mother's at it!

> DARREN
> *(looks at May)*
> Who cares! Get me a drink, for Christ's sake!

INT. SOHO. NIGHT

A crowded bar in Soho.

> BRUCE
> *(to May)*
> When I lost my wife I started collecting all the Penguins, then I went into older books. I've got some things from the seventeenth century . . . books that were made when Shakespeare was alive –

Bruce takes her hands.

May sees Paula kissing Darren now. Another man accidentally barges into them. Darren, who has become aggressive, starts to argue with him.

Paula pulls Darren away but only gets him as far as May, who puts her hand on his arm.

> MAY
>
> Darren, all right. Has something happened?

Darren shakes his head. May looks up to see Paula watching her hard.

> I think I'll go on one of my strolls. (*to Bruce*) Excuse me.

She goes. Bruce is alarmed.

> PAULA
>
> Let her go. She's almost a grown woman.

EXT. SOHO. NIGHT

May pushes through the busy street, packed with young people drinking.

EXT. PICCADILLY. NIGHT

May walks. She sits by the fountain. She walks. She sits. She thinks.

EXT. PICCADILLY. NIGHT

May looks up. Bruce is standing there.

> BRUCE
>
> It's all right.

> MAY
>
> Where's Paula?

> BRUCE
>
> With Darren. They don't want us oldies around.

INT. MANSION BLOCK. NIGHT

The stairs of Bruce's block of flats. May walking wearily up the wide stone stairs.

BRUCE

Can I help you?

MAY
(*reluctantly*)

Yes, yes, why not?

When he touches her for the first time she shivers.

INT. BRUCE'S FLAT. NIGHT

Now they are inside Bruce's 'old gentleman's' flat. Books; pictures; good furniture. He is fixing her a drink.

BRUCE

I can feel the world streaming past me – incomprehensibly, as it seems at my age. I feel left out; stupid. But she reads all my work and she's given me something meaningful to do. She's an inspiring teacher. How proud you must feel!

MAY

Yes, yes . . .

BRUCE

Are you tired, May?

MAY

So much has happened. There's so much to worry about. But I can't go back home. I'm not ready for old age.

BRUCE

Nor me, lovey.

MAY

But I don't know what I want to do.

BRUCE

I do.

INT. BRUCE'S BEDROOM. NIGHT

Later. Bruce ushers May into his bedroom.

INT. BRUCE'S BEDROOM. NIGHT

May watches Bruce undress. Braces, big underpants, vest.

He folds his clothes carefully. He turns to her and smiles.

> MAY
> What do you want me for?

INT. BRUCE'S BEDROOM. NIGHT

They are in bed and he is about to fuck her.

> MAY
> No, not in me!

> BRUCE
> Come on, please – just keep still!

Her distraught face as he fucks her. After:

> I needed that.

INT. BRUCE'S BEDROOM. NIGHT

Later. Bruce is asleep, snoring loudly. May gets out of bed quietly.

INT. BRUCE'S FLAT. NIGHT

May creeps out, careful not to wake Bruce.

In the hall, she pauses, picks up an ornament and lets it drop to the floor.

EXT. PAULA'S FLAT. NIGHT

May tries to unlock the door. She realises Paula has put the chain on. May bangs on the door.

> MAY
> Paula, Paula . . . oh please, please, it's cold.

The curtain moves and we see Paula's face behind the nets.

INT. PAULA'S FLAT. NIGHT

Paula, in her dressing gown, lets May in.

> PAULA
>
> I thought you weren't coming back.

> MAY
>
> Where would I be?

> PAULA
>
> Thought you might fancy a bit of Bruce.

> MAY
>
> Oh daughter, don't talk to me like that.

> PAULA
>
> Why, didn't you do it with him? I know you did, and Dad
> hardly in his grave.

Pause.

> I haven't been to bed.

Paula picks up a bottle of wine and takes a long drink from it.

> Something's disturbing me.

> MAY
>
> We'll talk about it tomorrow, I think I'll lie down.

> PAULA
> (*as May moves away*)
>
> Mother, I've taken your advice. I've given Darren a deadline
> and asked him to leave his wife and come and live here
> with me.

> MAY
>
> I see.

> PAULA
>
> He agreed.

> MAY
>
> He what?

PAULA

He said he would . . . he will come. He's going to tell her,
for fear I'll go there and tell her myself. When he comes
tomorrow, with his pathetic things in plastic bags, you'll
have to go. We'll be staying in a lot. I'll need to clear this
place out.

Pause.

Mother, do you love me?

MAY

Yes. Yes, I do. You're my daughter.

PAULA

You must be so happy about Darren and me.

INT. PAULA'S FLAT. NIGHT

*May, lying on the sofa, unable to sleep, realises there are flames at the
window behind her.*

EXT. YARD. NIGHT

*May rushes out to investigate. She finds that Paula, wearing a coat
over a nightdress, has made a bonfire, onto which she is throwing
manuscripts, papers, notebooks.*

MAY

Paula, what's this?

PAULA

My work. Years of it.

MAY

What are you doing with it?

PAULA

A little clear-out, I thought.

MAY

Now? Paula!

As Paula comes out with armfuls of manuscripts:

PAULA

Doesn't it make a pretty fire! (*She throws a manuscript on.*)
There goes a fine story! And a poem! Oops . . . there's a
play!

MAY

Why?

PAULA

You told me not to waste my time.

MAY
(*cries*)

Paula –

PAULA

I could find a better man, I could find better things to do,
everything could be better if I was a different and better
kind of person altogether. This is the way, this is the start –
of something else! I'm doing what you want me to do,
Mother. I'm doing what you asked! (*She throws another
stack of papers onto the fire.*)

INT. BOBBY AND HELEN'S KITCHEN. MORNING

May sits there distractedly with Bobby.

BOBBY

I'd go home if I were you.

MAY

I'm going into town.

BOBBY

I'm saying, back to your own house, to live. I can arrange
for you to have counselling, if you want.

MAY

Is that what people do instead of taking an interest in their
family?

BOBBY

What you do – you're more than grown-up – it's none of
my business, but I wouldn't mess around with Paula's
fragile head. And . . . Darren's easily distracted. He's kind
of strange, Mother . . . really.

MAY

Does he know you're selling the house and the
conservatory he's just done?

BOBBY

I haven't had time to discuss it with him.

MAY

I'd look to yourself, Bobby. To you and Helen. How did
you become so cold, my son?

BOBBY

How did you become so hot?

Darren comes into the room with a joint in his mouth.

DARREN

Bobby, darling –

BOBBY

Put that shit out! Listen to me, pal, if that job is not finished by when we said, I'm firing you and getting someone else to complete it. Okay? (*He looks at them both.*) This isn't a holiday camp!

DARREN

What's up with you?

BOBBY

Out, both of you! Get the fuck out!

Bobby storms out, slamming the front door.

INT. BOBBY AND HELEN'S CONSERVATORY. DAY

May and Darren sit together. Darren has just finished cutting out a line of powder. Now he snorts the drug and sits back with his legs apart.

DARREN

Bandersnatch! How about a little rub-a-dub, eh, Mother?

MAY

Please don't call me that.

DARREN

Feel me up. You know you like it. Get down.

She gets on to her knees.

MAY

Be tender with me, please.

DARREN

Oh, I am – I am, sometimes. But I like it when you're a
tarty old thing. You've got a dirty wet mouth. Put your
lipstick on and suck my cock in it.

MAY

I'll do anything, Darren, you know that, but please talk to me.

DARREN

Have you really got the money?

MAY

Yes!

DARREN

For us to travel and live there?

MAY

You know I have.

DARREN

Give it to me then.

MAY

I'm glad you're in a hurry. Will you tell your wife tonight?

DARREN

Tell her what?

MAY

That you're going.

DARREN

I never speak to that lunatic.

Pause.

You're always boasting about it, May, but where is the filthy
lucre, the dosh? How much have you actually got tucked
into your capacious bra there?

MAY

It'll be an airline ticket.

DARREN

What did you say?

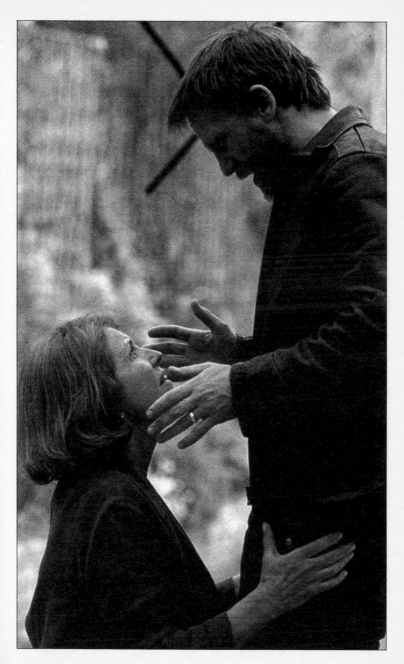

MAY

Darren, I said I'd buy you a ticket, because I care for you.
You won't be able to trade it in. You can only get on the
plane. With me.

DARREN

Plane? I've never been on a plane! I'm too mad to get on
a bus! I'd jump out of the window. You idiot – don't you
know anything?

MAY

How else are we going to get there?

DARREN

A ticket – what the fuck! Why should everyone have money
apart from me? They've all got cash in their pockets! What's
wrong with you all? Are you letting me down again after all
your promises! Are you trying to hurt me?

MAY

You make me want to do away with myself, Darren! What
have I done to make you angry? Hold me.

DARREN

Get off Paula!

MAY

Paula!

DARREN

What?

MAY

Don't you even know who I am?

DARREN

Who cares who you are, woman! I'm sick of all you women
pawing and clawing at me! No one does anything for me!
What am I, a prostitute, to listen to you and fuck you and
make you feel all right?

MAY

It's mutual!

DARREN

Mutual! I'm up to my neck in the shit with everyone!

MAY

Why?

DARREN

Paula knows what you've been doing to me!

MAY

She doesn't! How? Did you tell her?

DARREN

She's not a fool. That's why she's squeezing me, suddenly!
'Will you live here, will you live there!' She never leaves
me alone! You've both used me! I'm all over the place now!
How will I recover if people keep raping me!

He takes a tool and starts to hack the conservatory.

This is coming down! Break it up, break it up, break it up!

MAY

Stop it! Stop it! Darren, Darren, it's all right . . . okay, okay.

*She grabs him and holds him until he calms down. At last she kisses
him and gets up.*

INT. PAULA'S FLAT. DAY

*May sits alone. She stands. She walks about the kitchen. Picks up a
knife.*

She is on her knees holding the knife in front of her.

MAY

What have I done, Toots, since you left me?

*She holds the knife at her heart. Paula watches her through the crack
of the door.*

PAULA

You can have him.

May is shocked. Puts down the knife.

I've been badly betrayed. It's been horrific and I can't say I like you much, Mother. It isn't as if you've ever done more than the minimum for me, either . . . I seem to have lost everyone lately, father, lover, mother. But I'm still alive and there are things I want to know. What am I good at? What do I want to do? What do I like? What sort of men are there out there? What are the possibilities? Well, I'm going to find out . . .

MAY

Is there anything I can do?

PAULA

At last! Yes. There is. For days I've been thinking about it. There is one thing.

MAY

Oh tell me, tell me, Paula.

PAULA

I think . . . I think I want to hit you.

They look at one another.

Do you understand?

MAY

Paula . . .

PAULA

Yes, I think it would be a very good idea.

MAY

Now?

PAULA

It's as good a time as any.

Paula stands back to hit her. May lifts her head.

It'll be hard on me, leaving Darren. Worse for Jack. Still . . .

Paula strikes her, then:

INT. BOBBY AND HELEN'S HOUSE. DAY

Darren is working on the conservatory, repairing the part he smashed up. Bobby is with him.

Across the room, Helen is with an Estate Agent, who is measuring up.

> HELEN
> (*to Estate Agent*)
> It might not look like it, but it's nearly done –

> ESTATE AGENT
> It'll add considerable, considerable –

> HELEN
> I would hope so, after the disruption.

> ESTATE AGENT
> If the new people don't like it, they can knock it down.

> HELEN
> Of course they can!

Paula and May come into the room. May's face is damaged from Paula's blow. Helen sees them first.

> Oh God! What's happened?

They all look. Paula and May look at Darren.

> BOBBY
> (*to Darren*)
> Looks like the game's up, friend.

Now Helen is with May, examining her face. Bobby goes to May too.

> MAY
> It's not so bad. We had an argument. I've got the message.
> Now I'm going home.

> BOBBY
> Right. Okay. Oh, Mum! I'll give you a lift to Euston.

> MAY
> I'll take the Tube.

INT. BOBBY AND HELEN'S LIVING ROOM. DAY

May, with her bag, walks through the house. Darren with Paula looks up as May passes, and raises his hand. Paula is about to give Darren an earful.

INT. BOBBY AND HELEN'S HOUSE. DAY

In another room, the children are eating pizza and watching TV. They turn, briefly, to wave at their grandmother.

> HARRY
>
> Bye, Grandma!

> ROSIE
>
> Bye-bye!

They turn back to watch the TV.

INT. BOBBY AND HELEN'S HOUSE. DAY

Jack is dancing furiously.

INT. BOBBY AND HELEN'S HOUSE. DAY

In another room, Helen is tidying things away. She looks up at May and smiles.

> HELEN
>
> Goodbye, May.

INT. BOBBY AND HELEN'S HOUSE. DAY

At the end of the corridor. Bobby waves to his mother.

> BOBBY
>
> Bye-bye, Mother. Come again soon.

INT. TRAIN. DAY

May on the train back home, looking out of the window.

INT. SUBURBAN HOUSE. DAY

May sits at the kitchen table. On the table are Toots's slippers. May is very still.

INT. SUBURBAN HOUSE BEDROOM. NIGHT

May lies in bed. She turns and looks at the clock on the bedside table.

INT. SUBURBAN HOUSE. DAY

May is packing in her front room. Open suitcases, her clothes in piles, ready to go in. Also, beside her bag, money, passport, airline tickets.

EXT. STREET. DAY

May walks up the street, trundling her suitcase behind her.